PLATES *to* PLATTERS

recipes for small to large gatherings

pil

Publications International, Ltd.

Some of the products listed in this publication may be in limited distribution.

Pictured on the front cover: Ramen Antipasti Salad *(page 8)*.

Pictured on the inside front cover: Caprese Stuffed Zucchini Boats *(page 76)*.

Pictured on the inside back cover: Gemelli & Grilled Summer Vegetables *(page 48)*.

Pictured on the back cover *(clockwise from top left)*: Chicken, Hummus and Vegetable Wraps *(page 52)*, Pasta Salad *(page 75)*, BBQ Chicken Flatbread *(page 5)*, and Grilled Chicken with Corn and Black Bean Salsa *(page 47)*.

ISBN-13: 978-1-68022-738-3

Library of Congress Control Number: 2016952254

Manufactured in China.

8 7 6 5 4 3 2 1

TABLE *of* CONTENTS

APPETIZERS
and STARTERS

BBQ CHICKEN FLATBREAD

Makes 4 servings

3 tablespoons red wine vinegar

2 teaspoons sugar

¼ red onion, thinly sliced (about ⅓ cup)

3 cups shredded rotisserie chicken meat

½ cup barbecue sauce

1 package (about 14 ounces) refrigerated pizza dough

All-purpose flour, for dusting

1½ cups (6 ounces) shredded mozzarella cheese

1 green onion, thinly sliced on bias

2 tablespoons chopped fresh cilantro

1 Preheat oven to 400°F; set oven rack to lower third of oven. Line baking sheet with parchment paper.

2 Combine vinegar and sugar in small bowl. Add red onion; cover and let sit at room temperature. Combine chicken and barbecue sauce in medium bowl.

3 Roll dough into 11×9-inch rectangle on lightly floured surface. Transfer dough to prepared baking sheet.

4 Top flatbread evenly with cheese and barbecue chicken mixture. Bake about 12 minutes or until crust is golden and crisp and cheese is melted. Scatter pickled red onion over top. Garnish with green onion and cilantro. Serve immediately.

GOAT CHEESE CROSTINI WITH SWEET ONION JAM

Makes 24 crostinis

- 1 tablespoon olive oil
- 2 medium yellow onions, thinly sliced
- ¾ cup dry red wine
- ¼ cup water
- 2 tablespoons packed brown sugar
- 1 tablespoon balsamic vinegar
- 1 teaspoon salt
- ¼ teaspoon black pepper
- 2 ounces soft goat cheese
- 2 ounces light cream cheese, softened
- 1 teaspoon chopped fresh thyme, plus additional for garnish
- 1 loaf (16 ounces) French bread, cut into 24 slices (about 1 inch thick), lightly toasted

1 Heat oil in large skillet over medium heat. Add onions; cook and stir 10 minutes. Add wine, water, brown sugar, vinegar, salt and pepper; bring to a simmer. Reduce heat to low; cook, uncovered, 15 to 20 minutes or until all liquid is absorbed. (If mixture appears dry, stir in a few tablespoons of additional water.) Cool 30 minutes or cover and refrigerate until ready to use.

2 Meanwhile, stir goat cheese, cream cheese and 1 teaspoon thyme in small bowl until well blended.

3 Spread ½ teaspoon goat cheese mixture on each slice of bread. Top with 1 teaspoon onion jam. Garnish with additional thyme.

RAMEN ANTIPASTI SALAD

Makes 6 servings

1 can (13.75 ounces) whole artichoke hearts, drained, liquid reserved and cut in halves

1 package (3 ounces) chicken-flavored ramen noodles, coarsely crumbled

1 cup grape tomatoes, quartered

4 ounces fresh mozzarella balls

2 ounces hard salami, thinly sliced

½ cup pitted kalamata olives

¼ cup diced red onion

¼ cup fresh basil *or* 1 to 1½ tablespoons dried basil

¼ cup extra virgin olive oil

2 tablespoons cider vinegar

1 medium clove garlic, minced

½ teaspoon black pepper

¼ teaspoon red pepper flakes (optional)

1 Heat reserved artichoke liquid and ramen seasoning packet in medium saucepan to a boil over high heat. Add ramen noodles; reduce heat to medium. Cook 2 to 3 minutes or just until tender. (Noodles should absorb most of liquid.) Spread noodles on rimmed dinner plate or platter in thin layer to cool about 10 minutes. Drain excess liquid.

2 Combine artichokes, tomatoes, mozzarella, salami, olives, onion, basil, oil, vinegar, garlic, black pepper and red pepper flakes, if desired, in large bowl.

3 Add noodles to salad; stir gently to coat.

QUICK AND EASY STUFFED MUSHROOMS

Makes 16 mushrooms

1 slice whole wheat bread

16 large mushrooms

½ cup sliced celery

½ cup sliced onion

1 clove garlic

1 teaspoon Worcestershire sauce

½ teaspoon marjoram leaves, crushed

⅛ teaspoon ground red pepper

Dash paprika

1 Tear bread into pieces; place in food processor. Process 30 seconds or until crumbs are formed. Transfer to small bowl; set aside.

2 Remove stems from mushrooms; reserve caps. Place mushroom stems, celery, onion and garlic in food processor; process using on/off pulses until vegetables are finely chopped.

3 Spray large skillet with nonstick cooking spray. Add vegetable mixture; cook and stir over medium heat 5 minutes or until onion is tender. Remove to bowl. Stir in bread crumbs, Worcestershire sauce, marjoram and red pepper.

4 Fill mushroom caps evenly with mixture, pressing down firmly. Place about ½ inch apart in shallow baking pan. Spray tops with cooking spray. Sprinkle with paprika.

5 Preheat oven to 350°F. Bake 15 minutes or until heated through.

NOTE: Mushrooms can be stuffed up to 1 day ahead. Refrigerate filled mushroom caps, covered, until ready to serve. Bake in preheated 300°F oven 20 minutes or until heated through.

MINI MARINATED BEEF SKEWERS

Makes 18 appetizers

1 boneless beef top sirloin
  (about 1 pound)

2 tablespoons dry sherry

2 tablespoons soy sauce

1 tablespoon dark sesame oil

2 cloves garlic, minced

18 cherry tomatoes

   Lettuce leaves (optional)

1 Cut beef crosswise into ⅛-inch slices. Place in large resealable food storage bag. Combine sherry, soy sauce, sesame oil and garlic in small bowl; pour over beef. Seal bag; turn to coat. Marinate in refrigerator at least 30 minutes or up to 2 hours. Soak 18 (6-inch) wooden skewers in water 20 minutes.

2 Preheat broiler. Drain beef; discard marinade. Weave beef accordion-style onto skewers. Place on rack of broiler pan.

3 Broil 4 to 5 inches from heat 2 minutes. Turn skewers over; broil 2 minutes or until beef is barely pink in center. Place 1 cherry tomato on each skewer. Serve warm or at room temperature.

WONTON CHEESE AND SALSA CUPS

Makes 24 appetizers

Olive oil cooking spray

24 wonton wrappers

1½ cups (6 ounces) shredded
Cheddar or Monterey
Jack cheese

1½ cups salsa

1 Preheat oven to 350°F. Coat 24 mini (1¾-inch) muffin cups with cooking spray. Gently fit 1 wonton wrapper loosely into each cup. Spoon 1 tablespoon cheese into each cup.

2 Bake 8 to 10 minutes or until wontons are browned and cheese is melted. Transfer to wire racks. Spoon 1 tablespoon salsa into each cup. Serve immediately.

TIPS:

Salsa adds the unique flavor to these easy appetizers. Whether smoky chipotle salsa or fruity peach salsa, these bites will be a hit.

Tightly wrap remaining wonton wrappers. They will keep in the refrigerator up to 1 month and in the freezer up to 6 months.

For perfect cup-shaped appetizers, cut wontons into circles with 3-inch round cookie cutter. Gently flute the edges when placing into the muffin cups.

CROSTINI

Makes 16 appetizers

1 whole wheat mini baguette (about 4 ounces)

4 plum tomatoes

1 cup (4 ounces) shredded part-skim mozzarella cheese

3 tablespoons pesto sauce

1 Preheat oven to 400°F. Slice baguette into 16 very thin, diagonal slices. Slice each tomato lengthwise into 4 (¼-inch) slices.

2 Place baguette slices on ungreased baking sheet. Top each with 1 tablespoon cheese and 1 tomato slice.

3 Bake 8 minutes or until bread is lightly toasted and cheese is melted. Top each crostini with about ½ teaspoon pesto sauce. Serve warm.

SUMMER SALAD LETTUCE WRAPS

Makes 3 servings

¼ cup extra virgin olive oil

Juice of 1 lime

1 tablespoon red wine vinegar

1 cup grape tomatoes, halved

1 cup corn

½ cup diced fresh mozzarella cheese

¼ cup diced red onion

¼ cup chopped fresh basil

Salt and black pepper

6 crunchy lettuce leaves

1 Whisk oil, lime juice and vinegar in large bowl.

2 Add tomatoes, corn, cheese, onion and basil; toss to coat. Season with salt and pepper.

3 To serve, scoop ¼ cup salad mixture onto each lettuce leaf. Fold to eat.

MINI ASPARAGUS QUICHES

Makes 20 mini quiches

8 stalks asparagus

3 eggs

¼ teaspoon salt

¼ teaspoon black pepper

1 unbaked 9-inch pie crust

1 Preheat oven to 300°F. Spray 20 mini (1¾-inch) muffin cups with nonstick cooking spray.

2 Trim asparagus; thinly slice on the diagonal or coarsely chop enough to make ½ cup. Bring 3 cups water to a boil in medium saucepan. Add asparagus; cook 2 minutes over medium heat. Drain in colander; rinse under cold water.

3 Whisk eggs, salt and pepper in medium bowl; stir in asparagus.

4 Roll out pie dough into 13-inch circle. Cut out circles with 3-inch round biscuit cutter. Gather and reroll scraps to make 20 circles. Press circles into prepared muffin cups. Fill cups with egg mixture.

5 Bake 30 minutes or until tops are lightly browned and toothpick inserted into centers comes out clean.

MINI SWISS QUICHES: Prepare the muffin cups as directed, then whisk together 4 eggs, ¼ teaspoon salt and ¼ teaspoon black pepper. Stir in ¾ cup shredded Swiss cheese. Make dough circles as directed, and fill cups with egg mixture. Bake as directed. Makes 20 mini quiches.

BREAKFAST
and BRUNCH

WHOLE GRAIN FRENCH TOAST

Makes 4 servings

½ cup egg substitute *or*
    2 egg whites

¼ cup low-fat (1%) milk

½ teaspoon ground
    cinnamon

¼ teaspoon ground nutmeg

4 teaspoons butter

8 slices 100% whole wheat
    or multigrain bread

⅓ cup pure maple syrup

1 cup fresh blueberries

2 teaspoons powdered
    sugar

1 Preheat oven to 400°F. Spray baking sheet with nonstick cooking spray.

2 Whisk egg substitute, milk, cinnamon and nutmeg in shallow bowl until well blended. Melt 1 teaspoon butter in large nonstick skillet over medium heat. Working with two slices at a time, dip each bread slice in milk mixture, turning to coat both sides; let excess mixture drip back into bowl. Cook 2 minutes per side or until golden brown. Transfer to prepared baking sheet. Repeat with remaining butter, bread and milk mixture.

3 Bake 5 to 6 minutes or until heated through.

4 Microwave maple syrup in small microwavable bowl on HIGH 30 seconds or until bubbly. Stir in blueberries. Place french toast on 4 serving plates; top evenly with blueberry mixture. Sprinkle with powdered sugar.

PEACH PECAN UPSIDE-DOWN PANCAKE

Makes 6 servings

2 tablespoons butter, melted

2 tablespoons packed brown sugar

1 tablespoon maple syrup

½ (16-ounce) package frozen unsweetened peach slices, thawed

3 tablespoons pecan pieces

⅔ cup biscuit baking mix

2 eggs

⅓ cup fat-free (skim) milk

½ teaspoon vanilla

Additional maple syrup (optional)

1 Preheat oven to 400°F. Spray 9-inch pie pan with nonstick cooking spray.

2 Pour butter into prepared pan. Sprinkle with brown sugar and 1 tablespon maple syrup. Arrange peach slices in single layer over syrup. Sprinkle with pecans.

3 Place baking mix in medium bowl. Whisk eggs, milk and vanilla in small bowl; stir into baking mix just until moistened. Pour batter over peaches.

4 Bake 15 to 18 minutes or until lightly browned and toothpick inserted into center comes out clean. Cool 1 minute. Run knife around edge of pan. Invert pancake onto serving plate. Cut into 6 wedges. Serve immediately with additional maple syrup, if desired.

CRUSTLESS HAM AND ASPARAGUS QUICHE

Makes 6 servings

2 cups sliced asparagus (½-inch pieces)

1 red bell pepper, chopped

1 cup low-fat (1%) milk

2 tablespoons all-purpose flour

4 egg whites

1 egg

1 cup chopped cooked deli ham

2 tablespoons chopped fresh tarragon or basil

½ teaspoon salt (optional)

¼ teaspoon black pepper

½ cup (2 ounces) finely shredded Swiss cheese

1 Preheat oven to 350°F. Combine asparagus, bell pepper and 1 tablespoon water in microwavable bowl. Cover with waxed paper; microwave on HIGH 2 minutes or until vegetables are crisp-tender. Drain vegetables.

2 Whisk milk and flour in large bowl. Whisk in egg whites and egg until well combined. Stir in vegetables, ham, tarragon, salt, if desired, and black pepper. Pour into 9-inch pie plate. Bake 35 minutes. Sprinkle cheese over quiche; bake 5 minutes or until center is set and cheese is melted. Let stand 5 minutes before serving. Cut into 6 wedges.

VARIATIONS: Add 1 clove minced garlic. Add 2 tablespoons chopped green onion.

CHEESE BLINTZES

Makes about 14 blintzes

1 cup rice flour

¼ teaspoon salt

¼ teaspoon ground nutmeg

1 cup half-and-half

3 tablespoons butter, melted, divided

1½ teaspoons vanilla, divided

3 eggs

1 container (15 ounces) ricotta cheese

2 tablespoons powdered sugar

Preserves, applesauce or sour cream

1 Combine rice flour, salt and nutmeg in medium bowl. Gradually whisk in half-and-half until smooth.

2 Add 2 tablespoons butter and ½ teaspoon vanilla. Whisk in eggs, one at a time, until batter is smooth with the consistency of heavy cream.

3 Heat 8- or 9-inch nonstick skillet over medium heat. Brush lightly with some of remaining butter. Pour about ¼ cup batter into center of pan. Immediately swirl pan to coat with batter. Cook about 1 minute or until crêpe is dull on top and edges are dry. Turn and cook 30 seconds. Remove to plate; keep warm. Repeat with remaining batter.

4 Meanwhile, combine ricotta, powdered sugar and remaining 1 teaspoon vanilla in medium bowl. Fill crêpes with ricotta mixture. Serve with preserves, applesauce or sour cream.

INDIVIDUAL
SPINACH & BACON QUICHES

Makes 10 servings

3 slices bacon

½ small onion, diced

1 package (10 ounces) frozen chopped spinach, thawed and squeezed dry

½ teaspoon black pepper

⅛ teaspoon ground nutmeg

Pinch salt

1 container (15 ounces) whole-milk ricotta cheese

2 cups (8 ounces) shredded mozzarella cheese

1 cup grated Parmesan cheese

3 eggs, lightly beaten

1 Preheat oven to 350°F. Spray 10 standard (2½-inch) muffin cups with nonstick cooking spray.

2 Cook bacon in large skillet over medium-high heat until crisp. Drain on paper towels. Let bacon cool; crumble.

3 In same skillet, cook and stir onion 5 minutes or until tender. Add spinach, pepper, nutmeg and salt; cook and stir over medium heat 3 minutes or until liquid is evaporated. Remove from heat. Stir in crumbled bacon; set aside to cool.

4 Combine cheeses in large bowl. Add eggs; stir until well blended. Add cooled spinach mixture; mix well. Spoon evenly into prepared muffin cups.

5 Bake 40 minutes or until set. Let stand 10 minutes. Run thin knife around edges to remove from pan. Serve immediately.

BEIGNET WAFFLES

Makes 2 servings

1 cup pancake baking mix

⅔ cup milk

1 tablespoon vegetable oil

1 egg white

Juice of 1 lemon

2 tablespoons butter, melted

⅓ cup powdered sugar

⅔ cup assorted fresh berries
    or frozen berries, thawed

1 Preheat waffle maker to medium; lightly spray with nonstick cooking spray.

2 Whisk baking mix, milk, oil and egg white in large bowl. Pour ¾ cup* mixture onto waffle maker, close and cook 4 minutes or until puffed and golden brown.

3 Remove to plate; tent with foil to keep warm. Repeat with remaining batter. Cut each waffle into portions. Place on serving platter.

4 Squeeze lemon juice over waffles. Drizzle with melted butter; sift powdered sugar and spoon berries on top.

To make irregular-shaped waffles, reduce the mixture to ¼ to ½ cup.

SPINACH FETA FRITTATA

Makes 4 servings

1½ cups egg substitute

⅓ cup evaporated fat-free (skim) milk

1 package (10 ounces) frozen chopped spinach, thawed and squeezed dry

½ cup finely chopped green onions

1½ teaspoons dried oregano or basil

¼ teaspoon salt

⅛ teaspoon black pepper

2 cups cooked spaghetti (4 ounces uncooked)

4 ounces crumbled sun-dried tomato and basil or plain feta cheese

Diced red bell pepper (optional)

1 Preheat broiler.

2 Whisk together egg substitute and milk in medium bowl until well blended. Stir in spinach, green onions, oregano, salt and black pepper. Stir in spaghetti and feta cheese.

3 Spray medium cast iron or ovenproof skillet with nonstick cooking spray. Heat over medium heat. Add egg mixture; cook 5 minutes or until almost set, stirring occasionally.

4 Broil 3 to 5 minutes or until just beginning to brown and center is set. Cut into 4 wedges. Garnish with bell pepper.

FRITTATA WITH SUMMER VEGETABLES & HAM

Makes 4 servings

6 ounces extra-lean ham, thinly sliced and chopped

½ cup finely chopped green bell pepper

1 cup frozen corn, thawed

⅛ teaspoon ground red pepper

2 green onions, finely chopped

1 cup egg substitute

½ cup (2 ounces) extra sharp Cheddar cheese

1 Lightly coat medium nonstick skillet with nonstick cooking spray. Add ham; cook over medium-high heat 2 minutes or until beginning to brown, stirring frequently. Remove ham to separate plate.

2 Lightly coat same skillet with cooking spray. Add bell pepper; cook over medium-high heat 1 to 2 minutes, stirring frequently. Add corn and ground red pepper; cook 1 minute.

3 Stir in green onions and ham. Reduce heat to medium-low. Pour egg substitute evenly over all. Cover tightly and cook 8 minutes or until egg mixture puffs or just until edges begin to lightly brown.

4 Remove from heat. Sprinkle frittata with cheese. Cover; let stand 2 minutes to allow cheese to melt and eggs to set. Cut into 4 wedges to serve.

SERVING SUGGESTION: Serve with steamed or microwaved green beans and sliced tomatoes.

BANANA BREAD DOUGHNUTS

Makes 14 to 16 doughnuts

2¾ cups all-purpose flour

¼ cup cornstarch

1 teaspoon salt

1 teaspoon baking powder

½ teaspoon baking soda

½ teaspoon ground
  cinnamon

½ teaspoon ground nutmeg

½ cup packed dark brown
  sugar

2 eggs

¼ cup (½ stick) butter, melted

1 very ripe banana

1 teaspoon vanilla

½ cup buttermilk

½ cup finely diced very firm
  banana

  Oil, for frying

TOPPING

¼ cup whipping cream

½ cup bittersweet or
  semisweet chocolate
  chips

  Cinnamon-sugar (optional)

1 Whisk flour, cornstarch, salt, baking powder, baking soda, cinnamon and nutmeg in large bowl.

2 Beat brown sugar and eggs in large bowl with electric mixer on high speed 3 minutes or until pale and thick. Stir in butter, ripe banana and vanilla. Add flour mixture alternately with buttermilk, mixing on low speed after each addition. Fold in diced banana. Press plastic wrap directly onto surface of dough; refrigerate at least 1 hour.

3 Pour about 2 inches of oil into Dutch oven or large heavy saucepan; clip deep-fry or candy thermometer to side of pot. Heat over medium-high heat to 360°F to 370°F.

4 Meanwhile, generously flour work surface. Turn out dough onto work surface and dust top with flour. Roll dough about ¼ inch thick; cut squares with floured cutter. Cut 1-inch circles from center of squares with small cutter or top of small jar. Gather and reroll scraps. Line large wire rack with paper towels.

5 Working in batches, add doughnuts to hot oil. Cook 1 minute per side or until golden brown. Do not crowd the pan and adjust heat to maintain temperature during frying. Cool on wire racks.

6 Heat cream in small saucepan over medium-low heat until bubbles form around edge of pan. Stir in chocolate chips until smooth. Drizzle over doughnuts; sprinkle with cinnamon-sugar, if desired. Let stand until glaze is set.

CHEDDAR AND LEEK STRATA

Makes 12 servings

8 eggs

2 cups milk

½ cup porter ale or stout

2 cloves garlic, minced

¼ teaspoon salt

¼ teaspoon black pepper

1 loaf (16 ounces) sourdough bread, cut into ½-inch cubes

2 small leeks, coarsely chopped

1 red bell pepper, chopped

1½ cups (6 ounces) shredded Swiss cheese

1½ cups (6 ounces) shredded sharp Cheddar cheese

1 Spray 13×9-inch baking dish with nonstick cooking spray. Whisk eggs, milk, ale, garlic, salt and black pepper in large bowl until well blended.

2 Spread half of bread cubes in prepared baking dish; sprinkle with half of leeks and half of bell pepper. Top with ¾ cup Swiss cheese and ¾ cup Cheddar cheese. Repeat layers. Pour egg mixture evenly over top.

3 Cover tightly with plastic wrap or foil. Weigh down top of strata with slightly smaller baking dish. Refrigerate at least 2 hours or overnight.

4 Preheat oven to 350°F. Bake, uncovered, 40 to 45 minutes or until center is set. Serve immediately.

ENGLISH-STYLE SCONES

Makes 6 scones

3 eggs, divided

½ cup whipping cream

1½ teaspoons vanilla

2 cups all-purpose flour

2 teaspoons baking powder

¼ teaspoon salt

¼ cup (½ stick) cold butter

¼ cup finely chopped pitted dates

¼ cup golden raisins or currants

1 teaspoon water

6 tablespoons no-sugar-added orange marmalade fruit spread

6 tablespoons softly whipped cream *or* crème fraîche

1 Preheat oven to 375°F. Line large baking sheet with parchment paper.

2 Beat 2 eggs, cream and vanilla in medium bowl. Combine flour, baking powder and salt in medium bowl. Cut in butter with pastry blender or two knives until mixture resembles coarse crumbs. Stir in dates and raisins. Add cream mixture; mix just until dry ingredients are moistened.

3 Turn out dough onto lightly floured surface; knead four times with floured hands. Place dough on prepared baking sheet; pat into 8-inch circle. Gently score dough into six wedges with sharp wet knife, cutting three-fourths of the way through dough. Beat remaining egg and water in small bowl; brush lightly over dough.

4 Bake 18 to 20 minutes or until golden brown. Cool 5 minutes on wire rack. Cut into wedges; serve warm with marmalade and whipped cream.

BLUEBERRY PANCAKES

Makes 10 to 12 pancakes

2 tablespoons plus
     2 teaspoons unsalted
     butter

1¼ cups milk

1 egg, beaten

1¼ cups all-purpose flour

½ cup fresh blueberries

¼ cup packed light brown
     sugar or granulated maple
     sugar

1 tablespoon baking powder

½ teaspoon salt

   Powdered sugar *or* maple
   syrup

1 Melt butter in large skillet or griddle over medium heat. Pour into medium bowl, leaving thin film of butter on skillet. Whisk milk and egg into butter in bowl.

2 Combine flour, blueberries, brown sugar, baking powder and salt in large bowl; mix well. Add milk mixture; stir. *Do not beat.*

3 Pour batter into skillet, ¼ cup at a time. Cook over medium heat 2 to 3 minutes on each side or until golden. Dust with powdered sugar.

DINNERS and BBQS

GRILLED CHICKEN WITH CORN AND BLACK BEAN SALSA

Makes 4 servings

½ cup corn

½ cup finely chopped red bell pepper

½ of a 15-ounce can black beans, rinsed and drained

½ ripe medium avocado, diced

¼ cup chopped fresh cilantro

2 tablespoons fresh lime juice

1 tablespoon chopped sliced pickled jalapeño pepper

½ teaspoon salt, divided

1 teaspoon black pepper

½ teaspoon chili powder

4 boneless skinless chicken breasts (4 ounces each), pounded to ½-inch thickness

1 Combine corn, bell pepper, beans, avocado, cilantro, lime juice, jalapeño pepper and ¼ teaspoon salt in medium bowl. Set aside.

2 Combine black pepper, remaining ¼ teaspoon salt and chili powder in small bowl; sprinkle over chicken.

3 Coat grill pan with nonstick cooking spray. Cook chicken over medium-high heat 4 minutes per side or until no longer pink in center.

4 Serve chicken topped with half of salsa; refrigerate remaining salsa for another use.

47

GEMELLI & GRILLED SUMMER VEGETABLES

Makes 4 servings

2 large bell peppers (red and yellow)

12 stalks asparagus, trimmed

2 slices red onion

3 tablespoons plus 1 teaspoon olive oil, divided

6 ounces (2¼ cups) uncooked gemelli or rotini pasta

2 tablespoons pine nuts

1 clove garlic

1 cup loosely packed fresh basil leaves

¼ cup grated Parmesan cheese

¼ teaspoon salt

¼ teaspoon black pepper

1 cup grape or cherry tomatoes

1 Prepare grill for direct cooking. Cut bell peppers in half; remove and discard seeds. Grill bell peppers, skin-side down, on covered grill over medium heat 10 to 12 minutes or until skins are blackened. Place peppers in paper or plastic bag; let stand 15 minutes. Remove and discard blackened skins. Cut peppers into large pieces. Place in large bowl.

2 Toss asparagus and onion with 1 teaspoon oil in medium bowl. Grill on covered grill over medium heat 8 to 10 minutes or until tender, turning once. Cut asparagus into 2-inch pieces and coarsely chop onion; add asparagus and onion to peppers.

3 Cook pasta according to package directions; drain well and add to vegetables.

4 Combine pine nuts and garlic in food processor; process until coarsely chopped. Add basil; process until finely chopped. With motor running, add remaining 3 tablespoons oil; process until blended. Stir in cheese, salt and black pepper. Add basil mixture and tomatoes to pasta and vegetables; toss to coat. Serve immediately.

GRILLED PORK CHOPS WITH LAGER BARBECUE SAUCE

Makes 4 servings

1 cup lager

⅓ cup maple syrup

3 tablespoons molasses

1 teaspoon Mexican-style hot chili powder

4 bone-in, center-cut pork chops, 1 inch thick (2 to 2¼ pounds)

Lager Barbecue Sauce (recipe follows)

¾ teaspoon salt

¼ teaspoon black pepper

1 Combine lager, maple syrup, molasses, chili powder and pork chops in large resealable food storage bag. Marinate in refrigerator 2 hours, turning occasionally. Prepare Lager Barbecue Sauce.

2 Prepare grill for direct cooking over medium-high heat. Oil grid.

3 Remove pork chops from marinade; discard marinade. Sprinkle with salt and pepper. Grill 6 to 7 minutes per side or until 160°F. Serve with Lager Barbecue Sauce.

LAGER BARBECUE SAUCE

Makes ½ cup

½ cup lager

⅓ cup ketchup

3 tablespoons maple syrup

2 tablespoons finely chopped onion

1 tablespoon molasses

1 tablespoon cider vinegar

½ teaspoon Mexican-style hot chili powder

Combine lager, ketchup, maple syrup, onion, molasses, vinegar and chili powder in small saucepan over medium heat. Bring to a gentle simmer and cook, stirring occasionally, 10 to 12 minutes or until slightly thickened.

CHICKEN, HUMMUS AND VEGETABLE WRAPS

Makes 4 servings

¾ cup hummus (regular, roasted red pepper or roasted garlic)

4 (8- to 10-inch) sun-dried tomato *or* spinach wraps *or* whole wheat tortillas

2 cups chopped cooked chicken breast

Chipotle hot pepper sauce or Louisiana-style hot pepper sauce (optional)

½ cup shredded carrots

½ cup chopped unpeeled cucumber

½ cup thinly sliced radishes

2 tablespoons chopped fresh mint *or* basil

Spread hummus evenly over wraps all the way to edges. Arrange chicken over hummus; sprinkle with hot pepper sauce, if desired. Top with carrots, cucumber, radishes and mint. Roll up tightly. Cut in half diagonally.

VARIATION: Substitute alfalfa sprouts for the radishes. For tasty appetizers, cut wraps into bite-size pieces.

GRILLED SALMON FILLETS, ASPARAGUS AND ONIONS

Makes 6 servings

½ teaspoon paprika

6 salmon fillets (6 to 8 ounces each)

⅓ cup bottled honey-Dijon marinade or barbecue sauce

1 bunch (about 1 pound) fresh asparagus spears, ends trimmed

1 large red or sweet onion, cut into ¼-inch slices

1 tablespoon olive oil

Salt and black pepper

1 Prepare grill for direct grilling. Sprinkle paprika over salmon fillets. Brush marinade over salmon; let stand at room temperature 15 minutes.

2 Brush asparagus and onion slices with oil; season to taste with salt and pepper.

3 Place salmon, skin side down, in center of grill grid. Place asparagus and onion slices around salmon. Grill, covered, 5 minutes. Turn salmon and vegetables. Grill 5 to 6 minutes more or until salmon flakes when tested with fork and vegetables are crisp-tender. Separate onion slices into rings; serve over asparagus.

BBQ CHICKEN SALAD WITH ROASTED CORN AND CILANTRO

Makes 4 servings

2½ cups chopped cooked barbecue chicken*

½ cup corn niblets, roasted**

3 to 4 canned sweet roasted red peppers, chopped

2 green onions, chopped

¼ cup fresh cilantro, minced

2 tablespoons canola oil

2 tablespoons lime juice

1 teaspoon Dijon mustard

⅛ teaspoon black pepper

1 clove garlic, minced

Shredded cabbage (optional)

*Purchase barbecue roasted chicken breasts from the deli and remove the skin.

**Roast whole ear of corn on grill or place under broiler until browned. Frozen or canned corn niblets can also be used.

1 Combine chicken, corn, red peppers, green onions and cilantro in large bowl; gently mix.

2 Combine oil, lime juice, mustard, black pepper and garlic in small bowl; whisk well.

3 Spoon dressing over chicken mixture; carefully toss to bind ingredients.

4 Divide salad mixture into 4 portions; spoon onto shredded cabbage, if desired.

GRILLED FISH TACOS

Makes 4 servings

¾ teaspoon chili powder

1 pound skinless mahimahi, halibut or tilapia fillets

½ cup salsa, divided

2 cups packaged coleslaw mix or cabbage

¼ cup reduced-fat sour cream

4 tablespoons chopped fresh cilantro, divided

8 (6-inch) corn tortillas, warmed

1 Prepare grill for direct cooking. Sprinkle chili powder evenly over fish. Spoon ¼ cup salsa over fish; let stand 10 minutes.

2 Meanwhile, combine coleslaw mix, remaining ¼ cup salsa, sour cream and 2 tablespoons cilantro in large bowl; mix well.

3 Grill fish, salsa side up, covered, over medium heat 8 to 10 minutes or until fish is opaque in center and begins to flake when tested with fork.

4 Slice fish crosswise into thin strips or cut into chunks. Fill warm tortillas with fish and coleslaw mix. Garnish with remaining 2 tablespoons cilantro.

GREAT GRILLED BURGERS WITH SPINACH PESTO

Makes 4 servings

Spinach Pesto (recipe follows)

1½ pounds ground beef

¼ teaspoon salt

¼ teaspoon black pepper

4 to 8 slices provolone cheese

4 crusty Italian rolls, cut in half and toasted

4 to 8 slices tomatoes

Oak leaf lettuce

1 Prepare Spinach Pesto. Prepare grill for direct cooking.

2 Combine beef, ¼ cup pesto, salt and pepper in large bowl; mix lightly. Shape into 4 patties about ¾ inch thick. Reserve remaining pesto.

3 Place patties on grid over medium heat. Grill, covered, 8 to 10 minutes (or uncovered, 13 to 15 minutes) to medium (160°F) or to desired doneness, turning occasionally. Top each burger with cheese during last 2 minutes of grilling.

4 Spread remaining pesto on cut sides of each roll. Top bottom half of each roll with burger, tomato, lettuce and top half of roll.

SPINACH PESTO: Combine 2 cups spinach leaves, 3 tablespoons grated Romano cheese, 3 tablespoons olive oil, 1 tablespoon dried basil, 1 tablespoon lemon juice and 3 cloves garlic in food processor or blender. Process until smooth. Makes about ½ cup.

CHICKEN AND FRUIT KABOBS

Makes 12 servings

1¾ cups honey

¾ cup fresh lemon juice

½ cup Dijon mustard

⅓ cup chopped fresh ginger

4 pounds boneless skinless chicken breasts, cut into 1-inch pieces

6 fresh plums, pitted and quartered

3 firm bananas, cut into chunks

4 cups fresh pineapple chunks (about half of medium pineapple)

1 Prepare grill for direct cooking. Combine honey, lemon juice, mustard and ginger in small bowl; mix well. Thread chicken onto skewers,* alternating with fruit; brush generously with honey mixture.

2 Place kabobs on grill about 4 inches from heat. Grill 5 minutes on each side, brushing frequently with honey mixture. Grill 10 minutes more or until chicken is cooked through, turning and brushing frequently with remaining honey mixture.

If using wooden skewers, soak in water 20 minutes before threading with chicken and fruit.

CRISPY ORANGE VEGETABLES AND TOFU

Makes 4 servings

6 ounces spaghetti, uncooked

8 ounces firm tofu, drained and cut into 1-inch cubes

1 tablespoon reduced-sodium soy sauce

1½ cups vegetable broth or water

2 tablespoons cornstarch

1 tablespoon vegetable oil

2 cups sliced celery

1 cup broccoli florets

¾ cup red bell pepper chunks

⅓ cup sliced green onions

8 strips (1½×½ inch) orange peel

1 teaspoon minced fresh ginger

Orange slices (optional)

1 Cook spaghetti according to package directions; drain and keep warm. Meanwhile, combine tofu and soy sauce in medium bowl; set aside. Combine broth and cornstarch in cup; stir until smooth.

2 Heat oil in large nonstick skillet or wok. Add celery, broccoli, bell pepper, green onions, orange peel and ginger. Stir-fry 4 to 5 minutes until vegetables are crisp-tender. Stir cornstarch mixture and add to vegetable mixture; bring to a boil, stirring constantly until sauce thickens, about 1 minute.

3 Gently stir in tofu mixture; cook 1 minute or until heated through. Serve over spaghetti. Garnish with orange slices.

CALIFORNIA PICNIC LOAF

Makes 4 to 6 servings

1 (7- to 8-inch) round sourdough bread

¼ cup salsa

¼ cup mayonnaise or reduced-fat mayonnaise

½ cup (2 ounces) shredded Colby-Monterey Jack cheese

1 cup shredded romaine lettuce

2 cups chopped cooked chicken breast*

¼ cup sliced pitted black olives

1 avocado, thinly sliced

Use leftover rotisserie chicken or a 10-ounce package of cooked chicken.

1 Slice off top one third of bread, creating a lid; set aside. Scoop out bread insides from bottom of round, leaving a hollow shell. (Save bread insides for another use.)

2 Combine salsa, mayonnaise and cheese in medium bowl. Spread half on the bottom inside of the bread shell. Top with lettuce and layer with chicken and remaining salsa mixture. Layer olives and avocado. Press down for a firm filling. Cover with top lid of bread.

3 Wrap in plastic or foil and refrigerate up to 4 hours for easier slicing. When ready to serve, cut into 4 to 6 wedges.

TIP: Use leftover bread to make homemade croutons. Cut or tear into bite-size pieces, toss with a small amount of olive oil and dried herbs, spread onto a baking sheet and bake at 350°F for 10 to 12 minutes or until browned.

SESAME HOISIN BEER-CAN CHICKEN

Makes 8 to 10 servings

1 can (12 ounces) beer, divided

½ cup hoisin sauce

2 tablespoons honey

1 tablespoon soy sauce

1 teaspoon chili garlic sauce

½ teaspoon dark sesame oil

1 whole chicken (3½ to 4 pounds)

1 Prepare grill for indirect cooking over medium heat. Combine 2 tablespoons beer, hoisin sauce, honey, soy sauce, chili garlic sauce and oil in small bowl. Gently loosen skin of chicken over breast meat, legs and thighs. Spoon half of hoisin mixture evenly under skin and into cavity. Pour off beer until can is two-thirds full. Hold chicken upright with opening of cavity pointing down. Insert beer can into cavity.

2 Oil grill grid. Stand chicken upright on can over drip pan. Spread legs slightly to help support chicken. Cover; grill 30 minutes. Brush chicken with remaining hoisin mixture. Cover; grill 45 to 60 minutes or until chicken is cooked through (165°F). Use metal tongs to remove chicken and can to cutting board; let rest, standing up, 5 minutes. Carefully remove can and discard. Carve chicken and serve.

BEEF AND BLUEBERRY SALAD

Makes 4 servings

½ cup teriyaki sauce

¼ cup orange juice

¼ teaspoon hot pepper sauce

1¼ pounds lean boneless beef sirloin steak (1 inch thick)

8 cups sliced napa cabbage *or* bok choy

2 cups fresh blueberries

½ cup fresh red raspberries

½ cup raspberry vinaigrette salad dressing

1 Whisk teriyaki sauce, orange juice and hot pepper sauce in small bowl.

2 Place steak in large resealable food storage bag. Pour teriyaki mixture over steak; seal bag. Marinate in refrigerator at least 4 or up to 24 hours, turning bag occasionally.

3 Prepare grill for direct cooking.

4 Drain steak, discarding marinade. Grill steak over medium heat 8 to 12 minutes for medium rare, 12 to 16 minutes for medium or until desired doneness, turning once.

5 Remove steak to cutting board; let stand 4 to 5 minutes. Cut steak into very thin strips. Toss cabbage, blueberries, raspberries and steak pieces in large bowl. Drizzle with salad dressing.

BRATS 'N' BEER

Makes 4 servings

1 can (12 ounces) or bottle
  beer (not dark-colored)
4 bratwurst (about 1 pound)
1 sweet or Spanish onion,
  thinly sliced and separated
  into rings
1 tablespoon olive oil
¼ teaspoon salt
¼ teaspoon black pepper
4 sausage rolls

1 Prepare grill for direct cooking over medium heat.

2 Pour beer into medium heavy saucepan with ovenproof handle. Place saucepan on grid. Pierce bratwurst with knife; add to beer. Simmer 15 minutes, turning once.

3 Place onion rings on sheet of heavy-duty foil. Drizzle with oil; sprinkle with salt and pepper. Fold sides of foil over rings to enclose. Place packets on grid. Grill 10 minutes or until tender.

4 Transfer bratwurst to grid. Remove saucepan from grid; discard beer. Grill bratwurst 10 minutes or until browned and cooked through, turning once. Place bratwurst in rolls. Top with onion rings.

SALADS and SIDES

PASTA SALAD

Makes 8 servings

4 ounces uncooked spinach rotini or fusilli

⅓ cup finely chopped carrot

⅓ cup chopped celery

½ cup chopped red bell pepper

2 green onions with tops, sliced

3 tablespoons balsamic vinegar

2 tablespoons reduced-fat mayonnaise

2 teaspoons prepared whole grain mustard

½ teaspoon black pepper

¼ teaspoon Italian seasoning

Leaf lettuce

1 Cook pasta according to directions, omitting salt; drain. Rinse under cold running water until cool; drain.

2 Combine pasta, carrot, celery, bell pepper and green onions in medium bowl.

3 Whisk together vinegar, mayonnaise, mustard, black pepper and Italian seasoning in small bowl until blended. Pour over salad; toss to coat evenly. Cover and refrigerate up to 8 hours.

4 Arrange lettuce on individual plates. Spoon salad over lettuce.

CAPRESE STUFFED ZUCCHINI BOATS

Makes 6 servings

3 medium zucchini

1 package (3 ounces) ramen noodles, any flavor, broken into small pieces*

1 tomato, finely chopped

½ cup (2 ounces) shredded mozzarella cheese

2 tablespoons fresh chopped basil

1 tablespoon olive oil

1 clove garlic, minced

½ teaspoon salt

Discard seasoning packet.

1 Preheat oven to 375°F. Slice zucchini in half lengthwise; scoop out seeds, leaving the shell. Place in 2-quart baking dish.

2 Cook ramen noodles in boiling water 2 minutes; drain and place in large bowl. Add tomato, cheese, basil, oil, garlic and salt; stir to combine. Divide mixture among shells. Bake 25 minutes or until zucchini is browned and noodles are lightly browned.

CHEESY WALDORF SALAD

Makes 6 to 8 servings

⅓ cup mayonnaise or
   reduced-fat mayonnaise

1 tablespoon honey

1 tablespoon cider vinegar

4 small *or* 3 large apples,
   cored and cut into ½-inch
   pieces (about 4 cups)

4 ounces provolone cheese,
   cubed

2 stalks celery, thinly sliced

½ cup walnuts or pecans,
   toasted and chopped,
   divided

   Red leaf lettuce leaves

Combine mayonnaise, honey and vinegar in large bowl until blended. Add apples, cheese, celery and ¼ cup walnuts; stir to coat. (At this point the salad may be refrigerated up to 8 hours.) To serve, line individual salad plates with lettuce, then top with salad. Sprinkle remaining ¼ cup walnuts over each serving.

GREEN BEAN, WALNUT AND BLUE CHEESE PASTA SALAD

Makes 8 servings

2 cups uncooked gemelli pasta

2 cups trimmed halved green beans

3 tablespoons olive oil

2 tablespoons white wine vinegar

1 tablespoon chopped fresh thyme

1 tablespoon Dijon mustard

1 tablespoon fresh lemon juice

1 teaspoon honey

¼ teaspoon salt

¼ teaspoon black pepper

½ cup chopped walnuts, toasted*

½ cup reduced-fat crumbled blue cheese

To toast walnuts, spread in single layer in heavy-bottomed skillet. Cook over medium heat 1 to 2 minutes, stirring frequently, until nuts are lightly browned. Remove from skillet immediately. Cool before using.

1 Cook pasta according to package directions, omitting salt. Add green beans during the last 4 minutes of cooking. Drain. Transfer to large bowl.

2 Meanwhile, whisk oil, vinegar, thyme, mustard, lemon juice, honey, salt and pepper in medium bowl until smooth and well blended.

3 Pour dressing over pasta and green beans; toss to coat evenly. Stir in walnuts and cheese. Serve warm or cover and refrigerate until ready to serve.**

**If serving cold, stir walnuts into salad just before serving.

TANGY RICE, APPLE AND CABBAGE SLAW

Makes 6 to 8 servings

⅔ cup Celery Seed Vinaigrette (recipe follows)

2 cups water

2 teaspoons butter

¼ teaspoon salt

¾ cup uncooked long grain white rice

2 cups shredded red and green cabbage or prepared coleslaw mix

1½ cups chopped unpeeled tart red apples

½ cup chopped green onions

½ cup grated carrots

½ cup slivered almonds

1 Prepare Celery Seed Vinaigrette; set aside.

2 Bring water, butter and salt to a boil in medium saucepan over medium-high heat. Stir in rice. Reduce heat to low; simmer, covered, 20 minutes. Remove from heat. Let stand 5 minutes or until water is absorbed.

3 Combine cabbage, apples, green onions, carrots and almonds in large bowl. Add rice; mix well.

4 Stir in Celery Seed Vinaigrette; toss until well combined. Cover; refrigerate until ready to serve.

CELERY SEED VINAIGRETTE

Makes ¾ cup vinaigrette

½ cup vegetable oil

3 tablespoons honey

2 tablespoons white wine vinegar

1 teaspoon celery seed

¾ teaspoon dry mustard

Salt

Combine oil, honey, vinegar, celery seed and mustard in small bowl. Stir with wire whisk until well blended. Season with salt.

NOTE: Celery Seed Vinaigrette can be prepared up to 2 days ahead. Cover and store in refrigerator. Whisk before using.

SPICY GRILLED CORN

Makes 4 servings

2 tablespoons butter, softened

1 tablespoon chopped fresh parsley

2 teaspoons lemon juice

½ teaspoon salt

½ teaspoon black pepper

½ teaspoon red pepper flakes

4 ears corn, husks and silks removed

1 Prepare grill for direct cooking. Combine butter, parsley, lemon juice, salt, black pepper and red pepper flakes in small bowl. Brush mixture evenly over corn.

2 Place two sheets of foil (about 12×18 inches each) on work surface; center 2 ears of corn on each piece of foil. Bring up sides of foil; fold over top and edges to seal packets.

3 Grill packets over medium-high heat, covered, about 15 minutes or until corn is tender, turning once.

MESCLUN SALAD WITH CRANBERRY VINAIGRETTE

Makes 8 servings

DRESSING

⅓ cup extra virgin olive oil

3 tablespoons champagne vinegar or sherry vinegar

1 tablespoon Dijon mustard

¾ teaspoon salt

¼ teaspoon black pepper

SALAD

10 cups (10 ounces) mesclun or mixed torn salad greens

4 ounces goat cheese, crumbled

½ cup dried cranberries

½ cup walnuts or pecans, coarsely chopped and toasted*

To toast nuts, spread in single layer on baking sheet. Bake in preheated 350°F oven 8 to 10 minutes or until golden brown, stirring frequently.

1 For dressing, whisk oil, vinegar, mustard, salt and pepper in small bowl. Cover; refrigerate at least 30 minutes or up to 24 hours before serving.

2 For salad, combine salad greens, goat cheese, cranberries and walnuts in large bowl. Whisk dressing again and add to salad; toss until evenly coated.

GARDEN PASTA SALAD

Makes 8 servings

6 cups (about 12 ounces) cooked penne pasta

2 cups shredded cooked boneless skinless chicken breasts

¾ cup chopped red onion

¾ cup chopped red or green bell pepper

¾ cup sliced zucchini

1 can (4 ounces) sliced black olives, drained

1 teaspoon red pepper flakes

1 teaspoon salt (optional)

1 can (10¾ ounces) condensed reduced-fat reduced-sodium cream of chicken soup, undiluted

½ cup lemon juice

½ cup grated Parmesan cheese

½ cup chopped fresh basil (optional)

¼ cup chopped fresh parsley (optional)

1 Combine pasta, chicken, red onion, bell pepper, zucchini, olives, red pepper flakes and salt, if desired, in large bowl; toss lightly.

2 Combine soup and lemon juice in small bowl; mix well. Pour soup mixture over pasta salad; mix well.

3 Sprinkle with Parmesan cheese. Garnish with basil and parsley.

MARINATED TOMATO SALAD

Makes 8 servings

1½ cups white wine or tarragon vinegar

½ teaspoon salt

¼ cup finely chopped shallots

2 tablespoons finely chopped chives

2 tablespoons fresh lemon juice

¼ teaspoon white pepper

2 tablespoons extra virgin olive oil

6 plum tomatoes, quartered

2 large yellow tomatoes,* sliced horizontally into ½-inch-thick slices

16 red cherry tomatoes, halved

16 small yellow pear tomatoes,* halved (optional)

Sunflower sprouts (optional)

Substitute 10 plum tomatoes, quartered, for yellow tomatoes and yellow pear tomatoes, if desired.

1 Combine vinegar and salt in large bowl; stir until salt is completely dissolved. Add shallots, chives, lemon juice and pepper; mix well. Slowly whisk in oil until well blended.

2 Add tomatoes to marinade; toss well. Cover; let stand at room temperature 30 minutes or up to 2 hours before serving.

3 To serve, divide salad equally among 8 plates. Garnish with sunflower sprouts.

ASPARAGUS WITH NO-COOK CREAMY MUSTARD SAUCE

Makes 6 servings

2 cups water

1½ pounds asparagus, trimmed

½ cup plain nonfat yogurt

2 tablespoons reduced-fat mayonnaise

1 tablespoon Dijon mustard

2 teaspoons lemon juice

½ teaspoon salt

Grated lemon peel (optional)

1 Bring water to a boil in large skillet over high heat. Add asparagus; return to a boil. Reduce heat; cover and simmer 3 minutes or until crisp-tender. Drain.

2 Meanwhile, whisk yogurt, mayonnaise, mustard, lemon juice and salt in small bowl until smooth and well blended.

3 Place asparagus on serving platter; top with sauce. Garnish with lemon peel.

CREAMY COLESLAW

Makes 8 servings

½ cup reduced-fat mayonnaise

½ cup low-fat buttermilk

2 teaspoons sugar

1 teaspoon celery seed

1 teaspoon fresh lime juice

½ teaspoon chili powder

3 cups shredded coleslaw mix

1 cup shredded carrots

¼ cup finely chopped red onion

Whisk mayonnaise, buttermilk, sugar, celery seed, lime juice and chili powder in large bowl until smooth and well blended. Add coleslaw mix, carrots and onion; toss to coat evenly. Cover and refrigerate at least 2 hours before serving.

FARMERS' MARKET POTATO SALAD

Makes 6 servings

Pickled Red Onions
(recipe follows)

2 cups cubed assorted
potatoes (purple, baby
red, Yukon Gold and/or
a combination)

1 cup green beans, cut into
1-inch pieces

2 tablespoons plain nonfat
Greek yogurt

2 tablespoons white wine
vinegar

2 tablespoons olive oil

1 tablespoon spicy mustard

1 teaspoon salt

1 Prepare Pickled Red Onions.

2 Bring large saucepan of water to a boil. Add potatoes;
cook 5 to 8 minutes or until fork-tender.* Add green
beans during last 4 minutes of cooking time. Drain
potatoes and green beans.

3 Stir yogurt, vinegar, oil, mustard and salt in large bowl
until smooth and well blended.

4 Add potatoes, green beans and Pickled Red Onions
to dressing; gently toss to coat. Cover and refrigerate at
least 1 hour to allow flavors to develop before serving.

*Some potatoes take longer to cook than others. Remove individual
potatoes to large bowl using slotted spoon when fork-tender.*

PICKLED RED ONIONS

Makes about ½ cup

- ½ cup thinly sliced red onion
- ¼ cup white wine vinegar
- 2 tablespoons water
- 1 teaspoon sugar
- ½ teaspoon salt

Combine all ingredients in large glass jar. Seal jar; shake well. Refrigerate at least 1 hour or up to 1 week.

GERMAN FRUIT SALAD

Makes 8 servings

2 jars (16 ounces each) maraschino cherries, drained

2 cans (11 ounces each) mandarin oranges, drained

1 can (20 ounces) fruit cocktail, drained

1 container (16 ounces) sour cream

1 tablespoon mayonnaise

Chopped walnuts (optional)

2 large red apples, cut into bite-size pieces

2 bananas, cut into bite-size pieces

1 Combine cherries, oranges and fruit cocktail in large bowl.

2 Combine sour cream and mayonnaise in medium bowl; stir into fruit mixture. Add chopped walnuts, if desired; mix well.

3 Cover; refrigerate 2 hours. Add apples and bananas just before serving; mix well.

VARIATION: This recipe can also be made with low-fat sour cream and mayonnaise.

ZUCCHINI RIBBON SALAD

Makes 2 servings

2 medium zucchini

2 tablespoons chopped sun-dried tomatoes (not packed in oil)

2 teaspoons olive oil

1 teaspoon fresh lemon juice

1 teaspoon white vinegar

⅛ teaspoon salt

2 tablespoons shredded Parmesan cheese

1 tablespoon pine nuts, toasted*

To toast pine nuts, spread in single layer in heavy skillet. Cook over medium heat 1 to 2 minutes or until nuts are lightly browned, stirring frequently.

1 Cut zucchini into ribbons using vegetable peeler. Combine zucchini ribbons and sun-dried tomatoes in medium bowl.

2 Whisk oil, lemon juice, vinegar and salt in small bowl until well blended. Drizzle over zucchini and tomatoes; gently toss to coat.

3 Divide salad evenly between 2 serving bowls. Top with cheese and pine nuts. Serve immediately.

CHOCOLATE CHIP S'MORE BITES

Makes about 4 dozen s'mores

1 package (about 16 ounces) refrigerated chocolate chip cookie dough

¾ cup semisweet chocolate chips

¼ cup plus 2 tablespoons whipping cream

½ cup marshmallow creme

½ cup sour cream

1 Preheat oven to 325°F. Spray 13×9-inch baking pan with nonstick cooking spray.

2 Press cookie dough into prepared pan, using damp hands to spread dough into even layer and cover bottom of pan. (Dough will be very thin.) Bake 20 minutes or until light golden brown and just set. Cool in pan on wire rack.

3 Meanwhile, place chocolate chips in medium bowl. Microwave cream on HIGH 1 minute or just until simmering; pour over chocolate chips. Let stand 2 minutes; stir until smooth. Let stand 10 minutes or until mixture thickens.

4 Combine marshmallow creme and sour cream in small bowl until smooth.

5 Cut bars into 1¼-inch squares with sharp knife. For each s'more, spread scant teaspoon chocolate mixture on bottom of one square; spread scant teaspoon marshmallow mixture on bottom of second square. Press together to form s'mores.

OATS 'N' APPLE TART

Makes 8 servings

1½ cups quick oats

½ cup packed brown sugar, divided

1 tablespoon plus ¼ teaspoon ground cinnamon, divided

5 tablespoons butter or margarine, melted

2 medium sweet apples, such as Red or Golden Delicious, unpeeled, cored and thinly sliced

1 teaspoon lemon juice

¼ cup water

1 envelope (¼ ounce) unflavored gelatin

½ cup apple juice concentrate

1 package (8 ounces) reduced-fat cream cheese, softened

⅛ teaspoon ground nutmeg

1 Preheat oven to 350°F. Combine oats, ¼ cup brown sugar and 1 tablespoon cinnamon in medium bowl. Add butter and stir until combined. Press onto bottom and up side of 9-inch pie plate. Bake 7 minutes or until set. Cool on wire rack.

2 Toss apple slices with lemon juice in small bowl; set aside. Place water in small saucepan. Sprinkle gelatin over water; let stand 3 to 5 minutes. Stir in apple juice concentrate. Cook and stir over medium heat until gelatin is dissolved. *Do not boil.* Remove from heat and set aside.

3 Beat cream cheese in medium bowl with electric mixer at medium speed until fluffy and smooth. Add remaining ¼ cup brown sugar, ¼ teaspoon cinnamon and nutmeg. Mix until smooth. Slowly beat in gelatin mixture on low speed until blended and creamy, about 1 minute. *Do not overbeat.*

4 Arrange apple slices in crust. Pour cream cheese mixture evenly over top. Refrigerate 2 hours or until set.

ROCKY ROAD SQUARES

Makes 8 to 10 servings

2 pieces lavash bread, each 9½×11 inches

3 tablespoons melted butter

¼ cup packed brown sugar

4 ounces finely chopped bittersweet chocolate

¾ cup chopped raw whole almonds

1 cup mini marshmallows

Coarse salt, for sprinkling (optional)

1 Preheat oven to 350°F. Line baking sheet with parchment paper.

2 Brush both sides of each lavash with butter. Place side-by-side on prepared baking sheet. Top with brown sugar, chocolate, almonds and marshmallows.

3 Bake 12 minutes or until sugar and chocolate are melted, lavash is golden and crisp and marshmallows are toasted. Sprinkle lightly with salt, if desired.

4 Cool 5 minutes on baking sheet; transfer to wire rack. Cool completely. Cut into squares to serve.

GRILLED PEACHES WITH SPICY CREAM CHEESE TOPPING

½ cup (4 ounces) cream cheese, softened

1 tablespoon honey

¼ teaspoon ground red pepper

2 cups thawed frozen whipped topping

6 peaches, halved and pitted

¼ cup slivered almonds, toasted*

Fresh mint leaves (optional)

To toast almonds, spread in single layer in heavy skillet. Cook and stir over medium heat 1 to 2 minutes or until nuts are lightly browned, stirring frequently.

1 Prepare grill for direct cooking over medium-high heat. Spray grid with nonstick cooking spray.

2 Gently stir cream cheese in medium bowl until smooth. Whisk in honey and ground red pepper until well blended. Fold in whipped topping. Cover and refrigerate until ready to use.

3 Place peaches, cut sides down, on prepared grill. Grill, covered, 2 to 3 minutes. Turn over; grill 2 to 3 minutes or until peaches begin to soften. Remove to plate; let stand to cool slightly.

4 Arrange 2 peach halves, cut sides up, on 6 serving plates. Top evenly with spicy cream cheese topping and almonds. Garnish with mint.

SUMMER BERRY-CUSTARD PIE

Makes 8 servings

9 whole graham crackers

¼ cup egg whites

2 tablespoons butter, melted and cooled

1 cup low-fat (1%) milk

1 egg

½ cup sugar substitute*

3 tablespoons cornstarch

Pinch salt (optional)

1½ cups plain low-fat Greek yogurt

2 teaspoons vanilla

1½ cups fresh blueberries or raspberries (or a combination of both)

This recipe was tested using sucralose-based sugar substitute.

1 Preheat oven to 350°F. Spray 9-inch glass pie plate with nonstick cooking spray.

2 Place graham crackers in food processor and process until finely ground. Transfer to medium bowl and stir in egg whites and butter. Press mixture into bottom and up side of prepared pie plate. Bake 10 minutes. Cool completely.

3 For filling, combine milk, egg, sugar substitute, cornstarch, and salt, if desired, in medium saucepan. Cook over medium heat 5 to 8 minutes or until mixture comes to a boil and thickens, whisking constantly. Remove from heat; stir in yogurt and vanilla.

4 Spoon filling into crust. Press plastic wrap directly onto surface of filling. Refrigerate 4 hours or until firm. Top with berries just before serving.

BROWNIE BITES

Makes 2½ dozen cookies

1 package (about 18 ounces) refrigerated chocolate chip cookie dough with fudge filling in squares or rounds (20 count)

¼ cup unsweetened cocoa powder

1½ teaspoons vanilla, divided

1 package (about 16 ounces) refrigerated chocolate chip cookie dough

4 ounces cream cheese, softened

1 cup sifted powdered sugar

1 Spray 30 mini (1¾-inch) muffin cups with nonstick cooking spray. Place chocolate chip cookie dough with fudge filling in large bowl; let stand at room temperature about 15 minutes.

2 Add cocoa and ½ teaspoon vanilla to dough in bowl; beat with electric mixer at medium speed until well blended. Shape dough into 30 balls; press onto bottoms and up sides of prepared muffin cups. Refrigerate 1 hour.

3 Preheat oven to 350°F. Shape chocolate chip cookie dough into 30 balls; place each ball into dough-lined muffin cups. Gently flatten tops if necessary.

4 Bake 14 to 16 minutes. Cool in pans 10 minutes. Remove to wire racks; cool completely.

5 Beat cream cheese and remaining 1 teaspoon vanilla in medium bowl with electric mixer at medium speed, gradually adding powdered sugar until frosting is light and fluffy. Spoon heaping teaspoonful frosting onto each cookie.

NOTE: Brownie Bites are best served the day they are made; leftovers should be refrigerated.

GRILLED PINEAPPLE WITH CARAMEL DIPPING SAUCE

Makes 4 servings

25 unwrapped caramels
⅓ cup half-and-half
¼ teaspoon rum flavoring
1 ripe pineapple, trimmed and
   sliced into 8 (½-inch) slices

1 Place unwrapped caramels, half-and-half and flavoring in small saucepan. Cook over low to medium-low heat, stirring until sauce is thick and smooth. Keep warm until ready to serve.

2 Place pineapple on grid over medium heat. Grill 10 to 12 minutes or until pineapple softens and turns deeper yellow in color, turning once.

3 Place pineapple on cutting board; cut into bite-size pieces. Discard core pieces. Serve pineapple with caramel sauce for dipping or drizzle over pineapple before serving.

COCONUT MOTHER'S DAY CAKE

Makes 10 servings

1 package (about 15 ounces) white cake mix

1 can (about 13 ounces) light coconut milk

4 egg whites

1 container (16 ounces) vanilla frosting

2 cups flaked coconut

1 Preheat oven to 350°F. Spray two 8-inch round cake pans with nonstick cooking spray; line with parchment paper.

2 Beat cake mix, coconut milk and egg whites in large bowl with electric mixer at low speed 30 seconds. Beat at medium-low speed 2 minutes or until well blended. Divide batter evenly between prepared pans.

3 Bake 40 to 45 minutes or until toothpick inserted into centers comes out clean. Cool in pans 10 minutes. Remove to wire racks; cool completely.

4 Place one cake layer on serving plate; spread with vanilla frosting. Top with remaining layer; frost side and top of cake with remaining frosting.

5 Press coconut into frosting on top and side of cake.

SUMMERTIME FRUIT MEDLEY

Makes 8 servings

2 large ripe peaches, peeled and sliced

2 large ripe nectarines, sliced

1 large ripe mango, peeled and cut into 1-inch chunks

1 cup fresh blueberries

2 cups orange juice

¼ cup amaretto *or* ½ teaspoon almond extract

2 tablespoons sugar *or* 3 packets sugar substitute

Fresh mint (optional)

1 Combine peaches, nectarines, mango and blueberries in large bowl.

2 Whisk orange juice, amaretto and sugar in small bowl until sugar is dissolved. Pour over fruit mixture; toss to coat. Marinate 1 hour at room temperature, gently stirring occasionally. Garnish with fresh mint.

TRUFFLE BROWNIE BITES

Makes 3 dozen brownies

¾ cup plus ⅔ cup semisweet chocolate chips, divided

½ cup (1 stick) butter, cut into chunks

1⅓ cups sugar

3 eggs

1 teaspoon vanilla

1 cup minus 2 tablespoons all-purpose flour

½ teaspoon salt

¼ cup plus 2 tablespoons whipping cream

Colored sprinkles

1 Preheat oven to 350°F. Line 36 mini (1¾-inch) muffin cups with paper or foil baking cups.

2 Combine ⅔ cup chocolate chips and butter in large microwavable bowl. Microwave on HIGH 30 seconds; stir. Repeat as necessary until chips are melted and mixture is smooth. Let cool slightly.

3 Add sugar to melted chocolate mixture; beat until well blended. Add eggs, one at a time, beating well after each addition. Stir in vanilla. Add flour and salt; beat until well blended. Spoon batter into prepared muffin cups, filling three-fourths full.

4 Bake 15 minutes or until tops are firm to the touch. Cool in pans 5 minutes; remove to wire racks to cool completely.

5 Heat cream to a simmer in small saucepan over medium heat. Remove from heat; add remaining ¾ cup chocolate chips. Stir until chocolate is melted and mixture is smooth. Let stand 5 minutes to thicken.

6 Dip tops of brownies in ganache; return to wire racks. Decorate with sprinkles. Let stand 30 minutes or until ganache is set.

FAVORITE POTLUCK CARROT CAKE

Makes 12 to 15 servings

1 package (about 15 ounces) yellow cake mix

1 package (4-serving size) vanilla instant pudding and pie filling mix

3 cups grated carrots

1 can (8 ounces) crushed pineapple, undrained

4 eggs

½ cup chopped walnuts

½ cup water

2 teaspoons ground cinnamon

2 packages (8 ounces each) cream cheese, softened

½ cup (1 stick) butter, softened

2 teaspoons vanilla

2 cups powdered sugar, sifted

1 Preheat oven to 350°F. Spray 13×9-inch baking dish with nonstick cooking spray.

2 Combine cake mix, pudding mix, carrots, pineapple, eggs, walnuts, water and cinnamon in large bowl. Beat with electric mixer at low speed 30 seconds. Beat at medium speed 2 minutes. Pour batter into prepared dish.

3 Bake 40 to 45 minutes or until toothpick inserted into center comes out clean. Cool completely in dish on wire rack.

4 Beat cream cheese, butter and vanilla in medium bowl with electric mixer at medium-high speed 2 minutes or until fluffy. Gradually add powdered sugar, beating well after each addition. Spread over top of cake.

STRAWBERRY CREAM PIE

Makes 8 servings

- 1 cup plus 1½ teaspoons all-purpose flour, divided
- ¼ cup plus 1 teaspoon sugar, divided
- ¼ teaspoon salt
- ¼ cup (½ stick) cold margarine, cut into pieces
- 3 tablespoons ice water, divided
- ¾ teaspoon white or cider vinegar
- 6 ounces fat-free cream cheese
- 2 ounces Neufchâtel cheese
- ¼ cup vanilla fat-free yogurt
- 2 egg whites
- ½ teaspoon vanilla
- 1½ cups fresh strawberries, stemmed and halved
- ¼ cup strawberry jelly

1 Combine 1 cup flour, 1 teaspoon sugar and salt in medium bowl. Cut in margarine with pastry blender or two knives until mixture resembles coarse crumbs. Add 2 tablespoons ice water and vinegar; stir until moist but slightly firm dough forms. If necessary, add remaining 1 tablespoon ice water. Shape dough into a ball.

2 Preheat oven to 450°F. Roll out dough into 12-inch circle on lightly floured surface. Press dough into 9-inch glass pie plate; flute edge. Bake 10 to 12 minutes or until lightly browned. Cool on wire rack. *Reduce oven temperature to 325°F.*

3 Meanwhile, beat cream cheese, Neufchâtel, remaining ¼ cup sugar and 1½ teaspoons flour in large bowl with electric mixer at medium speed until creamy. Beat in yogurt, egg whites and vanilla until well blended. Pour into crust.

4 Bake 25 minutes or until set. Cool completely on wire rack. Arrange strawberries over filling. Melt jelly in small saucepan over low heat. Carefully brush glaze over strawberries, allowing glaze to run onto cheese mixture. Refrigerate 3 hours or overnight. Cut into 8 wedges.

METRIC CONVERSION CHART

VOLUME MEASUREMENTS (dry)

$1/8$ teaspoon = 0.5 mL
$1/4$ teaspoon = 1 mL
$1/2$ teaspoon = 2 mL
$3/4$ teaspoon = 4 mL
1 teaspoon = 5 mL
1 tablespoon = 15 mL
2 tablespoons = 30 mL
$1/4$ cup = 60 mL
$1/3$ cup = 75 mL
$1/2$ cup = 125 mL
$2/3$ cup = 150 mL
$3/4$ cup = 175 mL
1 cup = 250 mL
2 cups = 1 pint = 500 mL
3 cups = 750 mL
4 cups = 1 quart = 1 L

VOLUME MEASUREMENTS (fluid)

1 fluid ounce (2 tablespoons) = 30 mL
4 fluid ounces ($1/2$ cup) = 125 mL
8 fluid ounces (1 cup) = 250 mL
12 fluid ounces ($1 1/2$ cups) = 375 mL
16 fluid ounces (2 cups) = 500 mL

WEIGHTS (mass)

$1/2$ ounce = 15 g
1 ounce = 30 g
3 ounces = 90 g
4 ounces = 120 g
8 ounces = 225 g
10 ounces = 285 g
12 ounces = 360 g
16 ounces = 1 pound = 450 g

DIMENSIONS

$1/16$ inch = 2 mm
$1/8$ inch = 3 mm
$1/4$ inch = 6 mm
$1/2$ inch = 1.5 cm
$3/4$ inch = 2 cm
1 inch = 2.5 cm

OVEN TEMPERATURES

250°F = 120°C
275°F = 140°C
300°F = 150°C
325°F = 160°C
350°F = 180°C
375°F = 190°C
400°F = 200°C
425°F = 220°C
450°F = 230°C

BAKING PAN SIZES

Utensil	Size in Inches/Quarts	Metric Volume	Size in Centimeters
Baking or Cake Pan (square or rectangular)	8×8×2	2 L	20×20×5
	9×9×2	2.5 L	23×23×5
	12×8×2	3 L	30×20×5
	13×9×2	3.5 L	33×23×5
Loaf Pan	8×4×3	1.5 L	20×10×7
	9×5×3	2 L	23×13×7
Round Layer Cake Pan	8×1½	1.2 L	20×4
	9×1½	1.5 L	23×4
Pie Plate	8×1¼	750 mL	20×3
	9×1¼	1 L	23×3
Baking Dish or Casserole	1 quart	1 L	—
	1½ quart	1.5 L	—
	2 quart	2 L	—